AF483086

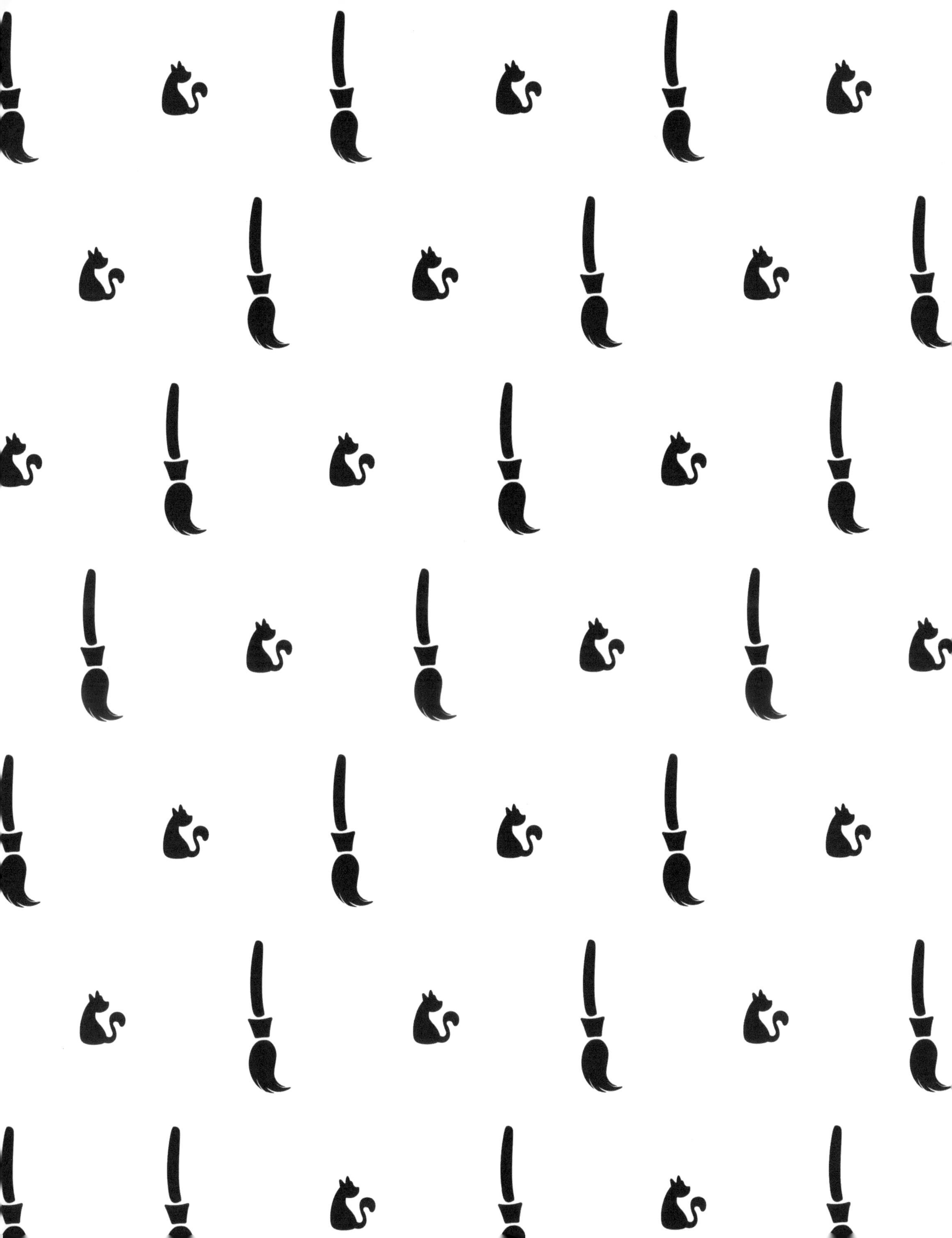

Willamina the Witch
Makes a Friend

Written by Luiza Jamkochian Supple

Illustrated by Anastasiia Kompaniiets

I dedicate this book to my beloved children, Julianna and Mason, whose boundless imaginations and unwavering spirits inspired this tale. May they forever cherish the joy of being their authentic selves.

"How lucky am I to be your mama".

Once upon a time in a small town where everyone
knew each other lived a young girl named Willamina.
To Willamina the town seemed perfect, but she
didn't feel like she fit in. She wore a black dress,
a cone-shaped hat, black pointy shoes, and rode a
broomstick.

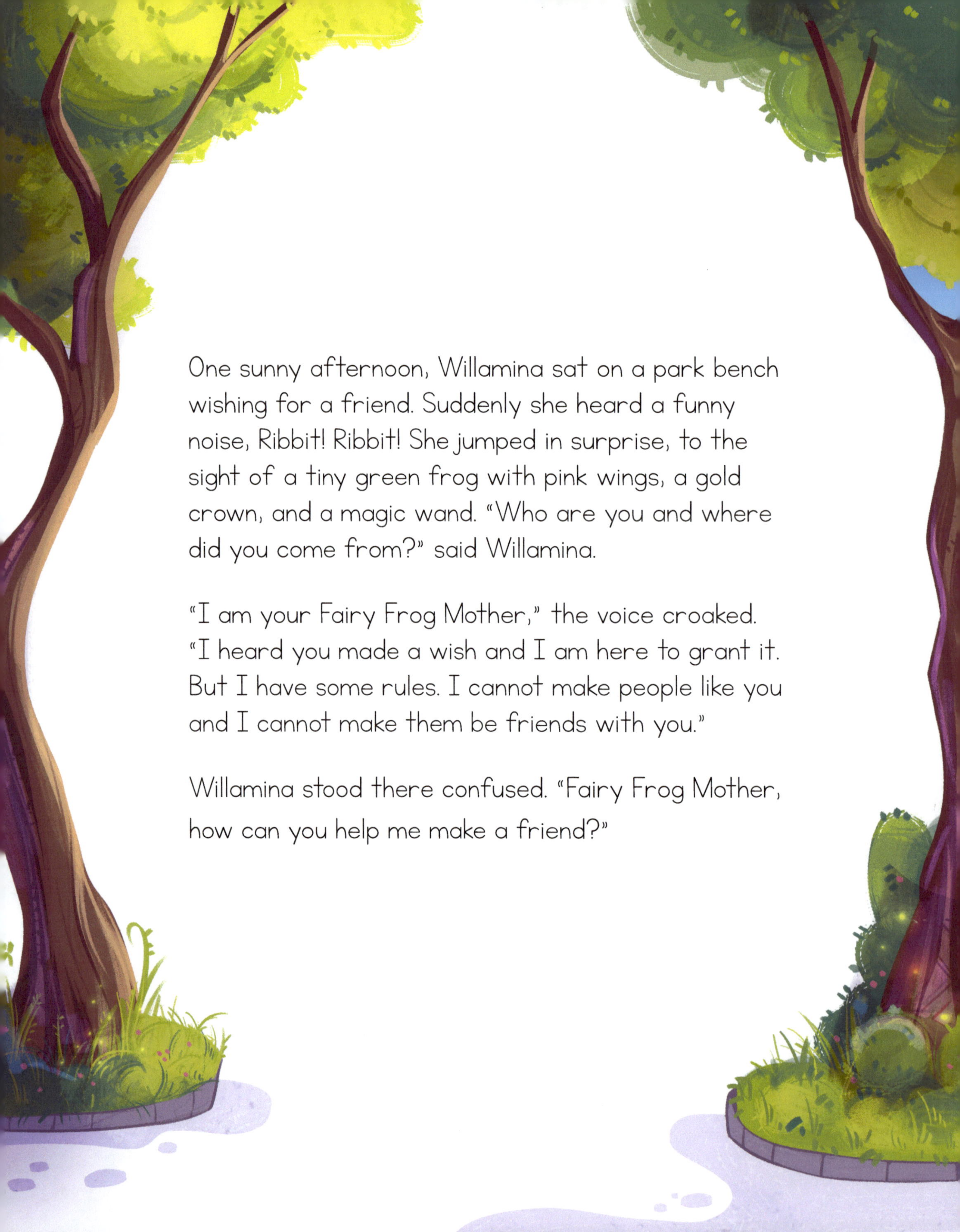

One sunny afternoon, Willamina sat on a park bench wishing for a friend. Suddenly she heard a funny noise, Ribbit! Ribbit! She jumped in surprise, to the sight of a tiny green frog with pink wings, a gold crown, and a magic wand. "Who are you and where did you come from?" said Willamina.

"I am your Fairy Frog Mother," the voice croaked. "I heard you made a wish and I am here to grant it. But I have some rules. I cannot make people like you and I cannot make them be friends with you."

Willamina stood there confused. "Fairy Frog Mother, how can you help me make a friend?"

"I'm so glad you asked. I have a few questions for you Willamina," said the Fairy Frog Mother. "What do you like to eat?"

Willamina smiled. "I love bat wings, frog legs...and oh! Spider webs! They're the best!"

"Those are...interesting choices," said the Fairy Frog Mother. "Maybe we could try pizza, french fries, or a grilled cheese sandwich? Other kids love those."

Willamina tried pizza: "Yuck, too saucy!"

Willamina tried french fries: "Yuck, too salty!"

Willamina tried a grilled cheese sandwich: "Yuck, too cheesy!"

Willamina sat there with a disgusted look on her face. The Fairy Frog Mother smiled. "Well, at least you tried them!"

MEN
Pizza....
French fries...
Sandwich...

"Let's try something else. What do you like to do for fun?" croaked the Fairy Frog Mother.

"That's easy! I like to scare people!" Willamina screamed with excitement.

Her Fairy Frog Mother seemed a bit confused. "Willamina, you won't make friends by scaring people. What if you tried something else? I hear kids your age like going to the trampoline park or for a bike ride."

Willamina took a moment to think, then yelled excitedly, "Let's go to the trampoline park!"

CAFE
TRAMPOLINE PARK

When Willamina got to the trampoline park, she saw all the other kids jumping, laughing, and having fun. She decided to give it a try. When she got on the trampoline, she jumped and jumped, soaring higher and higher until she lost control and came crashing down!

Willamina broke her favorite hat. "This is not for me! I will never come back to the trampoline park ever again!" cried Willamina. Sad and hurt, Willamina walked out of the trampoline park, dragging her broken hat behind her.

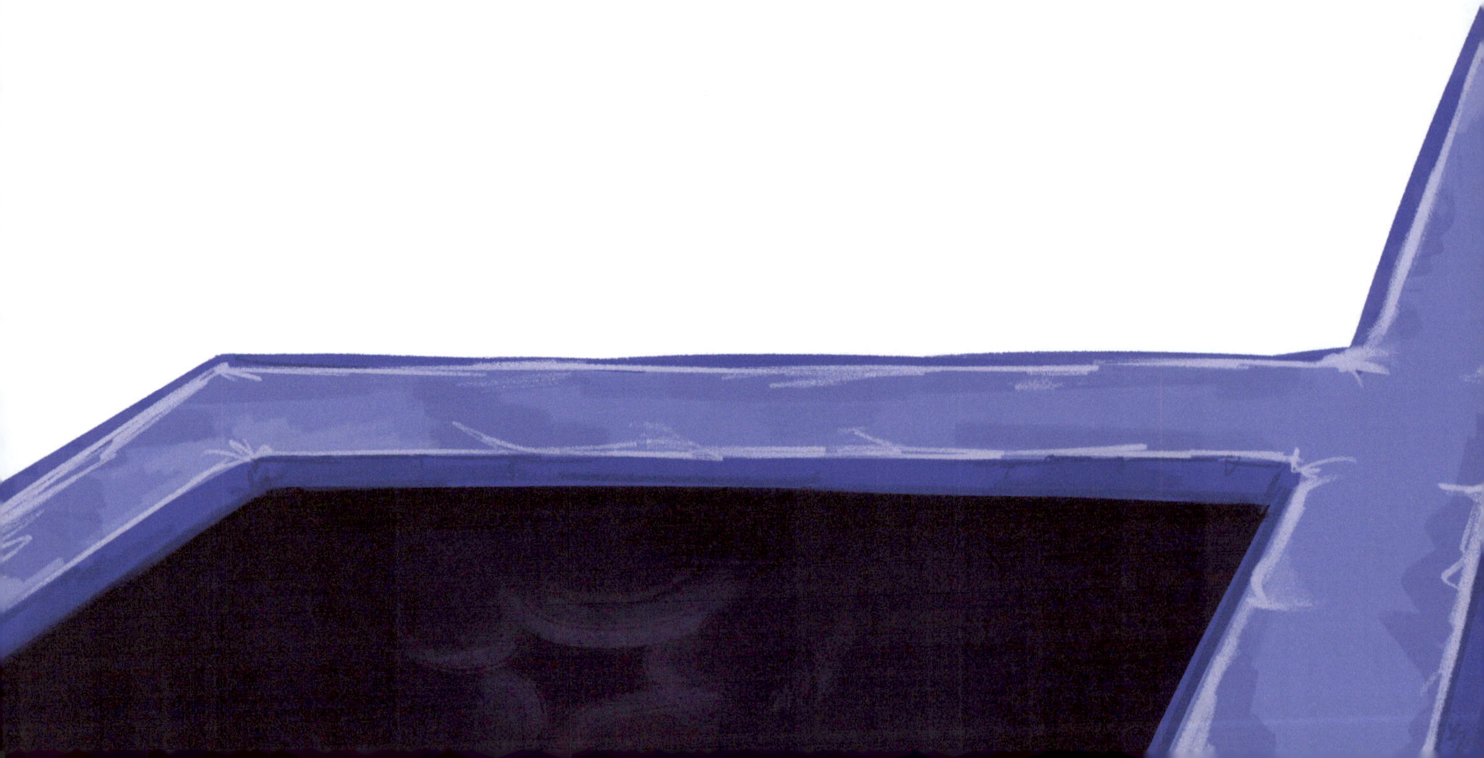

Her Fairy Frog Mother quickly came up with something else.
"It's such a nice day, Willamina. Let's go for a bike ride in the
park."

Willamina sighed, but agreed. "Why not? I can try riding
a bike. A bike can't hurt me or break my favorite hat." So
Willamina and her Fairy Frog Mother made their way to the
local park to ride bikes in the beautiful sunshine.

To Willamina's surprise, riding a bike was much harder than it looked. As she got settled on top of the bike, she started to wobble and lose control. She hit a rock on the path and flew off her bike, scraping her knee badly. "OUCH!" cried Willamina. "That hurt more than the trampoline park!

I will never ride a bike again!" She hopped on her broomstick and flew away, no pesky rocks could hurt her flying through the sky.

Her Fairy Frog Mother was running out of ideas. She suggested that Willamina try adding some colors to her wardrobe. Although hesitant, Willamina agreed, so they set off to the town square to do some shopping.

Willamina and her Fairy Frog Mother walked into a shop full of beautiful and colorful clothes. Willamina quickly found a bright pink skirt, a purple shirt, and rainbow socks. She was excited to try on all the new and wonderful colors."These are going to look amazing!" she squealed, rushing to try them on.

But when she twirled in front of the mirror, her smile faded. She didn't like what she was wearing. She didn't like it one bit. She didn't recognize who she saw in the mirror. She missed her black dress, her cone-shaped hat, her broomstick, and her black pointy shoes.

"This doesn't feel right. This is not who I am," said Willamina, feeling sad and ready to give up.

"Willamina decided it was time to go home. She said goodbye to her Fairy Frog Mother and thanked her for trying to help her make friends. Holding her broken hat and broomstick, Willamina waved goodbye to her Fairy Frog Mother as she boarded the bus.

"Willamina, you are perfect just the way you are," her Fairy Frog Mother called after her.

As Willamina was making her way down the bus aisle, she spotted another young witch wearing a familiar black dress, cone-shaped hat, and black shoes, with a broomstick in hand.

Willamina stopped and asked the young witch, "Is anyone sitting next to you?" The young witch was surprised that someone was speaking to her. All of a sudden, a bright smile spread across her face, and she replied, "No, this seat is saved for you!"

Willamina asked her fellow witch's name, and her new friend replied, "Winona!"

Right then, Willamina remembered what her Fairy Frog Mother had said: "Willamina, you are perfect just the way you are!" She realized that it wasn't about fitting in, but about finding the right friends who accept her for who she is.

Willamina and Winona were best friends from that bus ride onward.

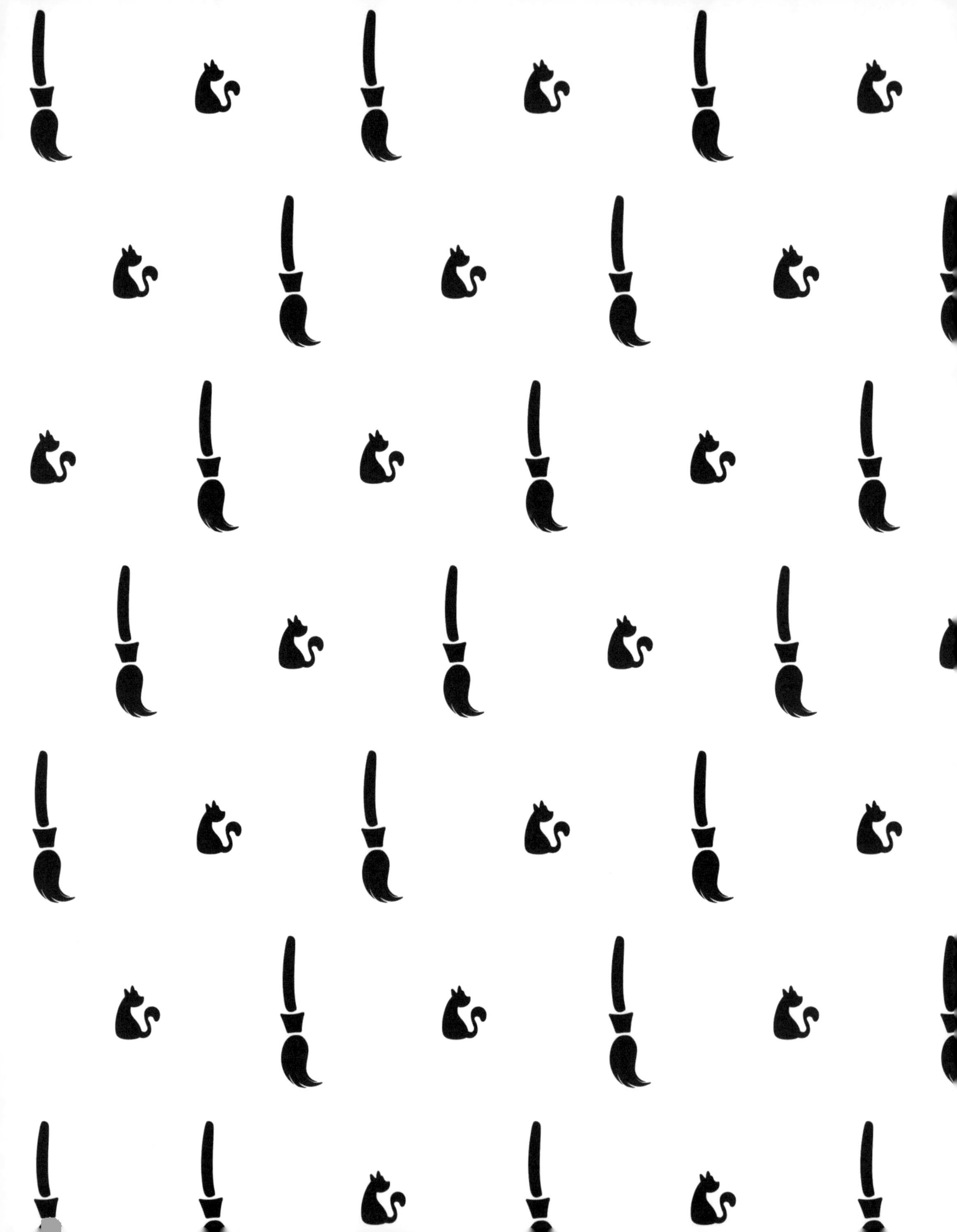